T0162088

THE CORONARY GARDEN

ALSO BY ANN TOWNSEND

Dime Store Erotics (1998)

The Coronary Garden

POEMS

Ann Townsend

Sarabande Books

LOUISVILLE, KENTUCKY

No part of this book may be reproduced without written permission of
the publisher. Please direct inquiries to:

Managing Editor
Sarabande Books, Inc.
2234 Dundee Road, Suite 200
Louisville, KY 40205

LIBRARY OF CONGRESS CATALOGING-IN-PUBLICATION DATA

Townsend, Ann, 1962–
The coronary garden : poems / by Ann Townsend. — 1st ed.
    p.   cm.
Includes bibliographical references.
ISBN 1-932511-10-5 (alk. paper) — ISBN 1-932511-09-1 (pbk. : alk. paper)
I. Title.
PS3620.O958C67 2005
811'.6–dc22   2004002727

Cover image: *Kelsey Plum.* Watercolor by Mary Daisy Arnold, 1912.
USDA Pomological Watercolor Collection. Special Collections,
National Agricultural Library.

Cover and text design by Charles Casey Martin

Printed in Canada through Four Colour Imports Ltd.
This book is printed on acid-free paper.

Sarabande Books is a nonprofit literary organization.

Partial funding has been provided by the Kentucky Arts Council, a state agency in the
Commerce Cabinet, with support from the National Endowment for the Arts.

FIRST EDITION

For K. G. B.

...as birds and trees and flowers without a name
all sighed when lawless law's enclosure came....

— John Clare, "The Moors"

TABLE OF CONTENTS

ACKNOWLEDGMENTS

My thanks to the editors of the following magazines in which these poems first appeared:

Crazyhorse: "From a Window"

Five Points: "Love Poem, Unwritten"; "The Wave"; "They Call You Moody"; "The Mowers"; "Cold Water"; "Early Days"; "No Shelter"; "Mindful of You"; "Old-Fashioned Kissing"

The Georgia Review: "The Coronary Garden"; "Preparatory Meditation"; "Touch Me Not"

Michigan Quarterly Review: "Candyland" (published as "Sleeping Child in a Rented Bed")

Mid-American Review: "Matters of Beauty"

The Missouri Review: "St. Veronica's Trials"; "Elegy"; "The Home Arts"

The Nation: "Fly Mask"

New England Review: "The Enclosure Act"

The Paris Review: "Childless"

Ploughshares: "As for Men"; "Mouse's Nest"

Poetry: "Ohio Farm House, ca. 1848"

The Southern Review: "The Dinner Guest"; "The Reliquary"

Southwest Review: "The Long Illness"

TriQuarterly: "Geraniums"; "A Door"

Witness: "Her Black Shoe"

"Butane, Kerosene, Gasoline" and "The Shirt Collar" first appeared in *The Bread Loaf Anthology of New American Poets* (University Press of New England, 2000). "Ohio Farm House, ca. 1848" was reprinted in *I Have My Own Song for It: Modern Poems About Ohio* (University of Akron Press, 2002). My thanks also goes to Denison University, for a Robert C. Good fellowship; to the MacDowell Colony, where this book was born; and to the National Endowment for the Arts, for a grant that supported the completion of this book.

ONE

The Coronary Garden

1.

What a fine package
you've come wrapped in.
A swathing of hospital cotton,

from the brisk whiteness   a tulip unfolding from
    each wrist.

A conduit, first here then there,
Your blood in its orbital system
circled safe in its chamber until

you let it out. Why did you let it out?

Plasma makes a great adhesive, a sticky blessing
between us. But I'm not the wounded one.
They stick   together, my fingers,

to the windowpane where I touch it.

2.

With tulips, "sometimes a rascally roote
produces a gallant flower."
And there are "some tawdry colors

that may be fringed with beauty." ·

My hand on the windowpane   it leaves a mark.
The blood makes it tacky.
A transport medium the doctor says,

rinsing his in the cleansing water.

Food, excrescence, lymphocytes, oxygen,
the red blood cells like cheerful donuts—
all on my hands

my hands a testament to your profusion

3.

And you oblivious
to the leakage we found together,
the doctor and me, him patching you,

me scooping up the shape the red assumes

as it coagulates into your palms,
into glue and glove,
the doctor shaking free of it,

and if I loved you better

would this mortal scene stay unwritten?
They "love an airy, moyst place," the tulips,
their fabulous tongues.

The flowers you choose for your coronary garden

4.

will crown your head when you die.
You grow the tulip "for it is the pearle
of the coronary garden," with ivy, vervain,

roses ferried from Egypt, asphodel,

any twining plant that might make a garland.
The garland   it rides out many occasions.
When Hippocrates cured the plague of Athens

by lighting fire to the city, the fuel therefore

was largely made of garlands.
Even a child may plait a garland.
Even a child can wear a light corona.

My hands   your blood beneath the nails

5.

like a red manicure.
Now your arteries are like a garden,
bacteria thriving there and blooming.

Are you drunk yet

on the failure of the systems?
Can your lungs support the fluid
as it gathers and collects?

Can your heart percolate?

The rue of your garden   it wards off drunkenness.
If I loved you more, wouldn't I have noticed
the grinding at the lip, the ataxia, you cumbered

by the darkness?

6

6.

Despair needles you with its whisper,
it is agnostic, it believes in irony,
like a fly's buzz it is perception, a busy

blood clot that says alive, alive.

I'm not the stopped motion, the straight line out.
Your garlands are "convivial, festival, sacrificial,
nuptual, honorary, funebrial."

That spring, when we strolled in the rain,

you bent to the stone wall's alyssum—
bloom, stem, and root, you tore a handful free.
Against your mouth the petals

were a mass of stars winking out.

7.

Now the heart beating in its wash,
nearly bled out.
Shall I braid a garland of rosemary, myrtle,

and what about apium,   also called celery,

which bears the metallic scent
of blood in its leaves?
Shall I bring you celery?

Outside the body blood doesn't belong

the doctor says.
You lay there whitely smiling.
If I loved you more

why would I want to taste it?

The Mowers

I'm looking at the intersection
    of thigh and cloth,
        oh at you,
where, caught in sunlight,
fabric adorns you.

Muscles shifting
    beneath skin, tendons
        maxed out at their task—
you're only scything
the field's fallow grass

down to stubble
    but I grow my fingernails long
        so they may graze you
and I paint them pink
to glow against your tan—

thigh to kneecap
    to the calf's demarcation.
        Who knows why
we love each other this way?
Your shout of laughter,

it arcs to me
        across the hillside
                where I weed away chicory,
other riffs of green
and the stinging

nettle, its rosary of pain.
        I press it against my palm
                and cross over to you,
bearing a stigmata,
red's rising tide.

They Call You Moody

Such proneness to sadness, such little fits
of life-grinding-to-a-halt:
today three diet cokes can't erase
the jack-pine limbs that dance maniacally
outside the window. All the world's
a pathetic fallacy where willows weep
and the two crows striding across the turf
freeze-frame into death's heads
with every snap of the camera's
imaginary stutter. Ha ha ha they caw
and carried on the updraft they soar and dip
against the sky's umbrella. Oh chemicals rich
in the blood, oh minor turbulent despair,
the sky unfolds, rinsed with bluing,
the crocuses snap open on their crazy
hinges. I hear it all, even through glass,
the loosening, the ticks, the groan.

Love Poem, Unwritten

My neighbor moving earth
on a cold day in August:
he has reamed a hillside
of shrubbery and tubers
and is filling it back up
with imported dirt. Until midnight
he swivels the rented earth-mover
and swears, and the engine
cuts through our conversation
like a dull persistent knife,
not going anywhere, not going
away. You want me
to write a poem to prove,
once and for all, my love for you.
In the sudden stillness
we hear our neighbor,
stumbling down from the tractor
and stabbing at the dirt
with a rake, or a shovel.
Something keeps me
from saying the words.
Could it be, I want to joke,
a genetic inability, my cold blood
clotting at the heart?

Then the stutter-start
of the earth-mover reminds me
of the night in the stalled elevator,
our first kiss, when my heart
jumped and skipped. The doctor
calls it abnormality,
just a mild cardiovascular
sickness, which I keep
in reserve, shyly hidden
in my shirt pocket,
like a stammering letter to you
that I fail and fail to send.

Elegy

His hands, specked and freckled
like an Irish trout, I wish
I could draw them. The nape of his neck,
hairless, mild. Whatever his smell,
that's gone now, too. Better perhaps
to count all the plates of eggs and toast
he ate at the New Orleans Riverbend—
that restaurant now defunct.
The waitress knew he did not favor grits.
She brought them anyway, in their own
ceramic bowl, with a pat of butter
wetly yellowing at the top.
What kind of love can only remember the menu?
It was years he pushed that bowl away.

Touch Me Not

*"Rembrandt went to extraordinary lengths to fix the
precise tone and bluish pallor of dead flesh...."*
— Simon Schama, *Rembrandt's Eyes*

They took my glasses and laid them

on a table. They took what rings
I wore. They raised my arm
above my head and I rocked against a pillow
that smelled sweet, like anesthesia,
like meat. I hoped to stay awake
for the operation, to see my thumb
flayed and spread apart
on the table, and pieced back together.
My arm was pinned and held
and treated kindly, rinsed and dried
and spoken to like a fearful dog.

That spring my father's hand in its death

looked like a claw, unhappily white,
and if I thought I saw a tremor,
a border flexing, it was just a shadow
resting on his finger's underside
and not his dumb hand beckoning to me.

15

I must have been crying by then.

His instrument raised the flexor tendons
from my wrist, and with swing music
in the background, the Vercet-induced
vapor and bright lights, I dreamed
"The Anatomy Lesson of Doctor Tulp"
as seen from below, from the dead man's
view, until finally my flayed hand and wrist
resembled a stringed instrument,
a tiny mandolin, tendons and ligaments
glistening in their residency.

For months before, chill air

surrounded my fingers like a traveling halo,
those I embraced flinched and said
touch me not. A marvel,
a magician's trick, a whiteness so dead cold
the doctor's temperature strip failed to register
at all. My love called me little ice cube.
My love opened jars for me
and brushed my teeth.

I wanted to reach in and I did,

to his thumb, flushed with embalming fluid.
I measured my own against it,
and like a paradox of motion and stillness,
Achilles running fast, and faster, going nowhere,
I floated my pulse upon silence
despite his pallor, every line of paint that brought him
forward, despite the unconstructed, awful hands
formed around a block, and pinned there.

Matters of Beauty

Though I read the hair of men
when scanned under microscopes
mirrors the matrix of my own hair
and though I've seen
a slender man rushing on a sidewalk,
long hair a flame
on his shoulders, and I was fooled,
and though the hair of my first love
fell into his eyes like a movie star's
and his lashes were equally long,
you are not him,
you are different from the rest,
stamped like a bronze coin
from earlier elements
now fallen out of favor
so your shorn head feels archaic,
bristling as it does
against my face each morning,
blades of grass cut clean
and shivered by the frost.
Soon, love, you'll be fifty.

As for Men

Days uncoiling like the hose
from her fingers, days
measured by the mechanical car
buzzing down the driveway.

Her boys wrestle for the control box,
their cries tear the air, hush the birds,
and send her, with hose, to transmit water
against their heads just enough to shut them off.

Now only the sound of the chastised car
scooting along, scraping ground in its metronome
of back and forth. Here in the calm,
the afterglow of punishment, she feels herself

soften again. The sun nurses the grass
to its greenness. It's a warm thumb
on her forehead. As for men, she likes
the warriors best, for instance in the movie last night

the one who hailed death, a missile,
who rose to greet it, an arrow in the chest.

Old-Fashioned Kissing

1.

Your mouth an oh of curiosity,
      your mouth's
courteous tongue touched mine—
      the rain
          against our faces,
the very small umbrella,
      and breakage   in the distance.

2.

But at that point
      I closed my eyes
to the distance.
      Your dangerous arm
          fitting neatly
      my waist,
your shoulder blades   like wings.

3.

They cut things, you said,
        when I stood behind you.
So I touched you.
        Is that a sign, you said.
                Your mouth
soft with kissing,
        my breathing   in agitation.

4.

I had to go home.
        I had to recover
my breath,
        hide it away, fasten the clasps
                of my loosened clothing.
        Oh skin, I said.
I lifted your sweater   anyway.

5.

I backed away. We drank water
        like there was no more water.
The glass was very clean.
        A quick kiss and goodbye.

Then again goodbye
at the doorway.
    Then some pleasant   wrestling

    6.

at your car.
    Never far from your hands
and their measured dance
    upon me,
       still I suffer
    the tug between our bodies,
the long distance   live wire.

The Long Illness

      Green accordions
expand at the base
of the geranium,

summer's last new leaves
an aromatica of pine
and stiff linen.

The stems' ropy arms
twist to an aspect
of devotion to the sun.

Without water I swallow
my pills, in sunlight,
force them down dryly,

my prayer to science.
Medicine, potion,
lozenge, all loosened

in the body's tissues:
the pills will outlast me.
And the geranium, supplicant,

twines around itself,
new leaves marking
the passage of the season.

Those come brightest
who come last, as I might flower,
myself, into something finer.

Just Toast, Thank You

Centered on the plate of eggs,
potatoes, toast, was a token
that told you: forget this life,
its mundane hungers.
It was only a lozenge
of ketchup balanced against
the plate's blue background,
a blot of pain like a sun
in winter sky, a bloodied eye.
But you stopped eating then,
spent your hours
attending to higher virtues,
the life of the mind, some call it.
In the background was that painterly figure,
washing dishes.
Yellow, yellow, yellow, the poet said,
love put its stain upon the world.

TWO

No Shelter

At the apex of a wet field,
a blackbird loops away from her nest

and a bucket filled with cracked corn and molasses
from my hand swings and stills.

The bird's yellow bars flame on the wind,
slice a circle from the air,
a neat scallop of space:

she wants me gone, and charts her course
until I cut past her, past the ridge line

to shake the grain
to the horses asleep

on the field spread out like a book
whose leaves are green,
whose words are writ in hard water.

Preparatory Meditation

Reading The Life of Wilfred, *I see how,*

when dying, he divided up his Church's
possessions: "I am making these decrees now
so that, when the Archangel Michael comes
to fetch me, he may find me prepared.
For the signs of death
are crowding thick about me."

Though daily life shut down

though air took on a yellow
cast, the smeared cream
of the pyres, though
they all grew sick together,
and though the tales of the plague years
were many, I remember best
the singer's tale,
who, solitary, sang mass on a street corner.

I'd like a drink

and a cigarette
he told my brother
but not with words
since he no longer
spoke.

When my father was dying

I sat on the steps of the enclosed garden
and let the light of the windows
fall on me. Women raging
in the kitchen—their voices
a shower of metallic threads
that settled over the garden
and coated it, trunk, bole,
and leaf, until the garden
was gleaming, from what
I cannot say, maybe
the iron light of despair.

The streets, emptied of people

or populated with bodies left
where they fell,

echoed His voice brick by brick.
But behind window shades
pulled against infection,
the pious listened from their second storeys.
Some lived, inexplicably.
Some died.

In the Haitian village

where he worked for a time nursing
each summer the same ailments
of the blood, the high cliffs disguise
the light, hide village from village
and the roads are only
illusions of sun and smoke and war.

My brother said no

not a cigarette
but I'll make you a drink
which he watered down
to just a cloud of scotch
in the clarifying water.

How many live here

he asked them
and their answer changed
by the day,
plus they counted their animals
as ones among them.

My mother said

with all the pain pills
wasn't he high, too high,
and Pat said no
I watered it down
and he lay back in bed
with a smile
he was so happy.

When the chickens were dying

dusting their wings spastically
into the ground,
and the children fell sick
with fever and blood blisters
and their parents after them,
he tried to explain contagion.

He stayed busy
killing fleas in their beds
while they called for the healer
who calmed the dying
with his song.
What a fantastic thought! —
invisible germs
flying through the night!

He said I did this

several times
in the last days
and he enjoyed it
it's what he wanted and why not.

Childless

A fallow field in January, crisping
under our boots; the red barn, slanting roof

that slumps and decays; the seed-stitching
of moles, their nocturnal habits,

humping the field in search of grubs;
the feathery lace of leaves on the ground;

the pebbled, fossilized dung of deer
strewn in the tall grasses—

we praise nature from the safety of our sweaters
while woodside a small figure runs from us,

dodging and weaving, invisible as the sound
of hissing. Is it a rabbit, dovetailing in the grass?

A farm cat, wilding? The ghost of our future?—
shadowing us, though we've left her behind.

Her Black Shoe

First the notes left
on her door's bulletin board,

then the trip-ups, nudges,
random stepping into her field

of privacy. He kept bumping
into her. He liked her eyes,

their American friendliness.
From Nowhere, U.S.A., he found

a home in her face.
Then it came to pass: she wandered

home from a dance,
there but not there, her mind fixed

on the pleasant flux and buzz
of her blood, awash with wine.

He swam into her sight
like an element of plot

a reader knows in advance
and turns from in despair.

He brought forth the next day's
dawn, the scraped hollow

in the road where they both stopped,
for a time. It was her eyes,

staring out of newsprint, already
yellowed, crisp, ready to be

tossed like trash, and the detail
of a shoe left behind

that he lingered over, with coffee,
for the days to come.

Your Body's Weight Upon Me

Exactly this moment and not another
I am clad in your sweater and my whitest skin,
your sweater being not yours exactly
but merely one upon which you placed
your hands and pushing it aside claimed
what was beneath. Exactly how you claimed me
is best left to the ellipses, the silent margins—
better to say

                    that in the market place
the vendor wraps his flowers in butcher paper
and twine, and ties the knot twice:
when you buy it you take it out into the cold.

Mindful of You

You followed, crept near,
rested your hand
on the slate windowsill
while voices fell
in boring incantation.
The smell of lilies spoiled the air.
It was a funeral but I was alive
to your hand which sent its pulse
across the short, sharp distance.
I wanted to lean into that hand.
I wanted to put my mouth to it.
I turned away reluctant from your light.
The mourners filled the space
with their shuffling, their dust.
They wished to take a last look
at the face that would soon
be no face. I never saw them.
It was a funeral
but I felt happy shame pressing
against my eyelids, same as you
who monitored the crowd,
steered me toward the coffin,
you whose fist, I saw, held crumpled
the commemorative card.

The Wave

Your death announced itself
            via the hotel telephone,
                        two short chirps

breaking the darkness of the bedroom.
            Surrounded as I was
                        by palms,

a shore breeze, it seemed
            like a silly joke you might
                        play, a ploy,

a disappearance, something faked
            for the money. At night
                        the sheets were perfumed

by the clams that burrow
            into the silt: after each wave
                        a lace of bubbles

serrates the sand, the pipers
            chase the waves, their slender beaks
                        the perfect size

to dart and probe, then dash on.
>   Then the news reached me
>   by e-mail, then

the door knocking, voices quick
>   with gossip. Innuendo, bad feelings
>   between us,

your enemies racing
>   to tell me first, and me
>   an enemy among them.

Next day I see your face
>   in the gloomy portrait
>   of Hawthorne

on the bookstore shelf.
>   His skin has reddened
>   from years of winter.

Even in the daguerreotype
>   the color bleeds through.
>   How many times

do I need to hear this song,
>   to replay it,
>   before I have it by heart?

Your gravesite is a measured plot,
    a wafer bearing your name:
        wave among waves.

A Door

In the clinic, the palsied boy thrashes
against his mother, who holds out the last

vestige of childhood, that he cannot see,
a rocking horse inside a clear bowl.

"Look," she pleads, while the therapist
persists at her lonely task, stretching

his arms past their limits, past their cramping
musculature, above his head. He's half-blind,

and his eyes explore the region of the ceiling
bright with pasted-on stars. His mother shakes

the toy to call him back, while those assembled
in the waiting room shudder through their pain

on plastic chairs, and the boy struggles
and shouts. All this takes place just beyond a door,

half-opened, that anyone may see, and know,
and warm themselves with their luck.

Butane, Kerosene, Gasoline

They fed the bonfire chips, chair legs,
and dark-grained deadfall gathered
from the woods. From upper windows

a rain shower swelled, billowed down
and was beer. Beneath their feet
the earth stirred. Their treble voices

were birdcalls displaced, shore birds
landlocked, a caterwaul, upheaval
against the stars' dense glittering.

Was it earthquake, midnight dynamite
or the heavy beat of their dancing?
In the pitch, the hard yaw of flames,

in sulfurous columns of smoke,
their faces flushed, dappled by mosquitoes
landing and feeding. Their anxious

voices: birdcalls burned alive,
scattered in a puff of feathers,
as some went to gaze drunken

at the stars, some to throw up
in the woods, some toward the house,
to supervise the burning of the beds.

The Reliquary

The world with its dangers
        submits to me,
my spells, my potions,
        for I outguess the heavens,
and with that blasphemy

which makes better my heart,
        I tap the seat belt,
the helmet, the pavement
        and other hard surfaces,
I carry a picture of you,

my purse a reliquary
        of your totems,
even when I forget you all day
        you're resident
in the smell of my clothes,

the bruises and scratches
        I bear for you,
that might be yours
        absent my intercedence,
and as for kitchen tools,

they're too dangerous altogether,
        I banish them for you,
let's eat out, yes,
        let's go now,
before it gets dark.

From a Window

Once, through the cloudless glass, you noticed
    a row of stars drifting west,

and reported that illusion to me —
    how they seemed to unhinge themselves

from their archaic stations
    and travel against all reason.

You thought your eyesight was giving way at last.
    You thought, for a minute, it was the invasion

we've all been waiting for.
    You passed one hand over your eyes.

And when you glanced back you saw
    the stars fixed finally in their hemisphere,

offering their variable light,
    and a single satellite, that had seemed

the only quiet, stationary star,
    marking its way in the everlasting sky.

THREE

The Dinner Guest

Let's begin with dinner, the menu:
      oiled lettuce, lemon juice, broken bread,

noodles spun with crushed tomatoes,
      and the matchstick julienne
            of fennel and skin of an orange.

I'm not angry yet, stirring the sauce.
      The wine tastes like a ripe field.

Let the fly rub his legs together
      over the wet cutting board,
            let him hold still in the bright aroma.

Dinner's next: sipping, chewing,
      talk of a high order among the men.

The female side of the table
      is motherly, leaning with spoons
            to serve the salad. No one says thanks—

is this 1953? Sorry.
      The newest year's dashed outside,

wind takes the trees,
>and pine needles fly, a dry shower,
>>a needle storm. There's no decorum outside.

Stirring, stirring more sauce,
>while his words cascade around me,

I focus on the spoon,
>ruined with red. The spoon
>>is the center of the rising heat world.

The spoon with its shreds of red
>holds the glory of taste and submission

in its olive grain.
>Bump, bump, bump, I tap the spoon
>>on the bowl's edge.

I keep undercutting the beauty.
>The guest is sated, sips his wine,

tips the chair on two legs.
>The fly has found the leftovers.
>>Let him eat from the same plate.

Ohio Farm House, ca. 1848

> *The glass-blue days are those*
> *when every color glows,*
> *each shape and shadow shows.*
> —Gerard Manley Hopkins

At least six cats called; dogs barked by every tree;
        iguanas, goats, lizards in a cage,
                spavined horse, then the pot-bellied pig

sniffed our shoes as we hung
        from the pasture fence,
                and the parakeet flew

room to room, our accompaniment
        in the blue house. The smell rose
                from plaster walls, from the dirt basement

where bees simmered in a nest, from the dark hole
        of the kitchen sink, from the mud room.
                It's that pee smell, the realtor said,

but she was wrong. The rich manure tea
        the farmer spread across the garden
                each spring wormed its way

beneath the fence, across the gravel yard,
        cataloguing, as it went,
                the molecules of age, decay,

the care and relief of the farmer who sat
        twenty feet away from that creeping
                spore-casting cloud beneath ground.

He carried a pole chair to the porch
        and rocked on those four legs.
                It's a still-life from above, or from

the receding point as we drive away.
        But beneath, it burns,
                and in a sun-sweat of garden earth

tomatoes writhe in their bath of steam,
        on multifoliate vines,
                and blossom.

Now the pig roots among them,
        his hocks sinking into earth;
                now he smells his own rude smell.

The Home Arts

I hold your face in my hands.
I can taste the cookie you fed me.
Do you know superfine sugar combusts
into butter as it melts?—so bakeries produce
a superior product the home cook
cannot aspire to. I am thinking
your nipple is very like a currant,
though not in its response to the tongue.
Many loves hover at the ceiling
as we smooth the one skin between us.
Then you remind me with your charming teeth
of the cascade of feeling that taste
brings alive: pain, sweetness,
a little tearing of the skin.
I let my eyes go soft focus
until you blur, until you burn off—
it's my only wish, to make age
pass away—like liquor
in the pan of plum sauce
set aflame.

St. Veronica's Trials

★ How she refused all food

With piteous smells hissing
            from her person
    she drove the sisters from her cell.
                The potions

of devils they said
            when she refused
    their aid in the form of an egg,
                threw it out

and would take no water. So she
            descended
    to absolute thinness,
                clamped her mouth

against bread, chewed the whole day
            on five
    orange seeds in praise of her master's
                five wounds.

Thereupon in contemplation
            of the oil of citrus

she lightheaded heard him call
her name.

How she wrote her autobiography under duress

The law for saints contains
its own
internal contradictions so she
penned

her story five times as proof
of sanity
though the ink dwelt
on her teeth

and she disliked writing
it took her
away from pondering
her winter

bruises and in any case
she altered
the stories each time
so who knew their

truth except for Him who provided
bread

never any more
            or less than needed.

★ *How she dreamt of the torments of the body*

Prayerful hours, marked by chimes,
            count her sleep
        in her cell, count the dreams
            as they keep

taunting her with tidings
            sent from hell, sent
        from the picture book of saints'
            laments,

she has them all: the fanged writhers,
            stones flung
        about to wake her, voices
            ripe and murmuring

words until she doubts her heart,
            the knives
        and sticks that pierce,
            the buzzing hives

and worst, the devils unspooling flesh
            from bone,

58

and bone, that white reminder,
                    that dead zone.

How the devil took her form in order to eat

She took to the kitchen
                    her appetite.
She took the food laid by
                    in casks.

She rode an apparition
                    wreathed in robes
that were not hers. She was
                    a manifestation,

breaking fast, eating in the corner
                    of the room.
She took off in flight
                    when caught.

She could not
                    be caught.
Her appetite made her
                    quick.

Go to the others and tell
                    this miracle.

Inscribe it in the register
                    of names.

★ *How she was tested by her confessor*

In her cell the walls
                    were speaking.
            She kept licking
                    the view.

On her tongue were hundreds
                    of abrasions.
            All the taste buds
                    were bowls of blood.

The mortar pressed its palm
                    into her mouth.
            Her confessor stood
                    behind her.

You have done me
                    a great favor, she cried.
            I have found the spiders
                    and they were good.

She licked the corners
                    and their webs.

They said penance
          hand in hand.

Early Days

I held her loosely swaddled
and she swallowed in my arms,

her breathing like a bellows
through the blankets,

hands tensing the air, each finger
articulated, thumbs longer

than the rest, all of her not four pounds,
then her tongue, forward as a kitten's,

curled and reached for milk,
which was given, and her eyes

darted in their sockets, still sealed
and much like an amphibian

long underwater,
the saturated texture of her skin

translucent, veined, prone
to bruising, yet urgent

to furl herself forward
into the mortal elements,

despite belonging, as she once did,
to the closed, amniotic world.

Geraniums

As if their rough fans had too much
of the light, the geraniums "fail to thrive,"

as one mother said of her frail baby,
reporting with some confusion the doctor's term.

What does it mean, she asked, and I had
no good answer but raised the infant

to be weighed and measured once again.
He hung between my hands like an empty

pocketbook, leathery, limp, his abdomen
paling where I held him. All summer,

despite our watering and tender care, the flowers
wilted. I watched the boy die, leaf by leaf.

I kept wishing I had something else
to turn to for the comparison.

The Shirt Collar

Out of the least shift in the wind,
out of the hitch and sway of it
through the bedroom window, the lace collar shivers

and falls from the dressmaker's dummy
like scrap paper. Now my quick daughter,
who wants to wear it just herself,

holds up this relic of the bygone,
unfolded and smoothed and petted-over.
It's like the trellis that sustains

the mildewed roses as they climb along
the window's ledge. But her hands in play
spell roughness, and the lace tears open,

undone strings. Together we spread the damage
on the floor, to realign the collar's wings,
tactile yarnovers and openwork,

and imagine what neck held the collar
coupled from behind, what white lawn, what gloves,
what swallowing in sunlight. Bent like this,

misbraided and flyaway curls,
she can't reshape the failing light
of the afternoon back into flowers.

They speak from the window their beauty,
their ill-health. And the dressmaker's dummy leans
in mute regard, bare-necked, skirts fluttering

around the machinery. If she had arms,
they might reach, gather her in, back
from what's unfeathering on the floor.

Candyland

Your hair, at night,
still tangled from your bath

and damp where it meshes
with the pillow, smells of shampoo

and the rusty water of the summer house,
and some sanctimony, some biblical

remnant cast down from the cross
hanging next to the rented bunk bed.

The window's open to the lake's heart
where no breeze but a dock light shines

and in the bathroom I cut my hair,
a fall, a white river, until it drops

in sheaves to the sink.
Asleep, tabulating dreams,

you send out armies of syllables
in a cloud so like cold weather

they nearly steam in the room
whose swells are warm

with piety and little plastic toys
that gather in the corners.

How will I measure
the blood that rises and falls

under the cusp of the ear? It isn't wings
furled against the back, it isn't

the rose leaf's beetle-eaten brocade.
Your hair, at night, caught

in shadow like so many threads
running through a waterfall,

weaves the frivolous air until
at daybreak, above a deadfall

of flies' wings clustered
in the corner of the room, you push it

away from your eyes. Released
from captive sleep, you rise.

Mouse's Nest

after John Clare

All dark, and my feet against
        the feed room floor
                scuff cement, find their way
        to the light,

the switch, which flares on
        with a snap of bird-
                wings' nimble shuffle
        and flight, the rafters

blowing off feathers,
        then my hands against
                the grain bin's aluminum lid,
        lifting it,

the sweet molasses
        inhalation,
                and the mice unfold
        in the sudden burn,

a nest of them,
        new ones still hanging on
                to the mother's teats
        as she rings the bin

with her fear
   and as each falls away, grain
     takes them, soft ones,
   all spinning skin and squeak

until, no way out,
   she stops and stares up
     at me, stilled above her,
   as if to ask

a question,
   babies now abandoned
     to the chaff; she doesn't hear them
   but fixes

her round red eyes on me,
   her eyes just like
     the crimson-topped pushpins
   in my heart-shaped

pincushion,
   but hers pulse with real life
     and that is the viscera,
   where revolt

begins as the work of wings
   in the throat

so with a shudder
my hand apprehends

the scoop
and spoons them furiously out
the open door,
into snow melt,

first light, grains scattering
with the bodies,
grain wriggling with the life
that feeds on it.

My breath's a scattershot,
an arrow, her answer.
Now, breeze:
silence wisping in the barn.

Sometimes the Horse

1. Night Ride

What are my hands
    as the twilight arrests us?
        Each bodily form
            fades with the sun.

If all my limbs were as tongues
    and those tongues
        could speak
            I would praise the horse

who says with her body,
    muscle, mouth, and bone,
        that leaves are old
            and turn each hour,

that field and fall's footsteps
    shower
        on our heads,
            that the hunter's in his blind

on a mantle
    of blood-rusted branches,

bow primed
for each movement, each mark,

a thousand sensory fields
honed
to the wind's
broken word.

2. FLY MASK

Today I come upon her weeping,
        gray face gone pewter.
                She holds still for me
                      and the wet sponge

pressed gently down,
        and closes her eyes.
                Beneath her skin the muscle ripples
                as a pond does

under water's pressure.
        So I put it on, to know
                what the horse sees
                      caged in the blue mesh,

in a realm of monocular vision.
        Rowing outward,
                past the screen that windows the view,
                are shadows,

field's edge, an island of trees.
        I fasten it beneath the throat
                while she chews the grain,
                      lips roving in the bucket.

Winter flies beyond the cage,
    pressing against my skin,
        whatever antennae I had
            lost in the generations.

3. Cold Water

Sometimes the horse
        dances above the jet of water,
                hooves with their sawdust

dropping and lifting as she dodges the hose.
        Sometimes she bears it,
                water from the well dousing

her coat, sweat and stain
        coursing groundward,
                a runnel, a river, her dapple coat dripping.

Wet mouth, she takes the pear
        from my hand and chews like a metronome
                counting down the warm days

as they fall. Around us
        wasps tap the door frame,
                hungry for the juices that linger at her lip.

Sometimes the horse bends earthward,
        not lips only, but whole body gone
                to gravity's pull,

then hocks down, belly down, all angles, she rolls.
And the earth takes us back, the water,
the dust, each bodily form.

The Enclosure Act

She examined the swampland and desired to drain it.

Her realtor's sign was a noble gesture on the roadside,
like a heraldic banner of the society of homes.

She had the capacity of mind to visualize, as they say, the
    end result.

Stipple leaf, wild rose, briar, briar, minnows,
quack grass, volunteer corn, an errant empty beer bottle,
    prairie remnant,
the soft depressions left where the plow passed,
the squeak sound of the realtor's sign elaborating in the
    wind.

What she saw were ranch condos fledged by white fencing,
and on and on. She had a capacity for longing, and an urge
    to fill it up.

A bird lit on the sign, bounced twice, and flew.
She was gaining weight, at this rate.

She could feel her stomach pressing against the buttons of
    her jeans.

At this rate, the jive of the wind would make a pasture of
    it. She saw it fenced,
the fence imposing a human face on the land.

Her boots sank in the mud. Time to fill it up.

Notes

"The Coronary Garden": The quoted material on flowers is taken from letters by Sir Thomas Browne to John Evelyn, as well as from John Evelyn's *Elysium Britannicum of the Royal Gardens,* edited by John E. Ingram. This treatise on gardens was written in the 17th century but only published in its entirety in 2001. One chapter, which Evelyn proposed but never got around to writing, focused on coronary gardens, whose flowers were grown in order to be fashioned into garlands, wreaths, or other "crowns."

"St. Veronica's Trials": I learned much about St. Veronica from Rudolf Bell's *Holy Anorexia,* a study of medieval visionaries and the connection between spirituality and eating disorders. Veronica Orsola's story is one of the case studies that Bell presents, and the poem borrows some of its details from this book.

The title "Your Body's Weight Upon Me" is adapted from a line by Edna St. Vincent Millay, as is the line "I turned away reluctant from your light," in "Mindful of You."

THE AUTHOR

ANN TOWNSEND is the author of *Dime Store Erotics* (1998). Her poems have appeared in such magazines as *Poetry, The Paris Review, The Nation, Witness, The Georgia Review,* and many others. She is the recipient of a National Endowment for the Arts Fellowship, an Individual Artist's grant from the Ohio Arts Council, and a Discovery Prize from *The Nation.* Her poems have been reprinted in many anthologies, including *The Pushcart Prize XX, The New Young American Poets, American Poetry: The Next Generation,* and *The New American Poets: A Bread Loaf Anthology.* An Associate Professor of English at Denison University, she lives in Granville, Ohio.